THE BOOK OF
BOND

THE BOOK OF
BOND

Alastair Dougall

CONTENTS

I admire your courage, Miss, er… Trench. Sylvia Trench. I admire your luck, Mr… **Bond. James Bond.**

Dr. No ™

MI6's chief agent in the Caribbean, John Strangways has disappeared. M dispatches Bond to Jamaica to investigate. Surviving several murder attempts, Bond travels to Crab Key, island stronghold of the enigmatic Dr. No. In this tropical paradise, Bond encounters beauty, in the form of shell diver Honey Ryder, and fiendish cunning, in the shape of SPECTRE mastermind Dr. No himself.

You're booked on the seven o'clock plane
to Kingston. That gives you exactly three hours
twenty minutes… I want to know what's
happened to Strangways.

M

BOND'S
NEW GUN

A shock awaited Bond before he left for Nassau to investigate Strangways' fate. M announced that instead of the Beretta Bond had used for ten years, he would be taking another gun, a Walther PPK. Bond protested that he had never missed with the Beretta, but M replied that the Beretta had jammed on Bond's last job and Bond had spent six months in hospital in consequence. The Walther PPK would be Bond's faithful companion through many missions.

If you carry an OO number, it means you're *licensed* to kill not *get* killed... You'll carry the Walther.

M

On the
BEACH

Bond landed on Crab Key, Dr. No's island, under cover of darkness. After a few hours rest, he was awakened, not by the roar of the isle's fabled dragon, but by a gentle calypso, sung by a siren in a white bikini. Her name was Honey Ryder.

What are you doing here?
Looking for shells?
No. I'm just looking.

Honey and **Bond**

MEETING DR. NO

Captured, detoxed and dressed for the occasion, Bond and Honey finally met the malevolent owner of Crab Key in his inner sanctum. There was a reason for Dr. No's show of amity. He was impressed by Bond's attempts to destroy his organization. To salve his hurt pride, Dr. No boasted about his scientific knowledge, his criminal genius and his plans to sabotage the US space programme. He even offered Bond a position in SPECTRE, which Bond was happy to reject.

Unfortunately, I misjudged you. You are just a stupid policeman whose luck has run out.

Dr. No

Dr No greeted his guests with stiff courtesy: "Forgive my not shaking hands... a misfortune."

FROM RUSSIA WITH L❦VE™

A Russian cipher clerk, Tatiana Romanova, claims to have fallen in love with a picture of James Bond. She wishes to defect, bringing with her a precious Lektor decoding machine. Bond meets her in Istanbul, arriving in the midst of a tit-for-tat war between MI6 and the KGB. With help from MI6's chief Istanbul agent Kerim Bey, Bond escapes on the Orient Express with Tatiana and the Lektor. He then discovers that he has been ensnared in a SPECTRE plot to destroy him personally and discredit MI6.

Arm or no arm –
I have to pull that trigger.

Kerim Bey

FATAL SHOT

Kerim Bey, head of Station T, was out for vengeance. The KGB assassin Krilencu had blown up his office and shot him in the arm during a gun battle at a gypsy camp. Kerim knew that Krilencu had a secret escape route concealed by a movie poster on the side of his house. As Kerim's policemen sons flushed Krilencu out, the wounded Kerim took aim with Bond's sniper's rifle.

Krilencu's escape hatch was situated in the mouth of actress Anita Ekberg, as depicted on a poster for the Bob Hope film *Call Me Bwana*.

WITH LOVE from
RUSSIA

Years as a Double-O agent had trained James Bond to be permanently on guard, ready for any eventuality. But even he was unprepared for his first encounter with Tatiana "Tania" Romanova. The beautiful Soviet defector had lured him to Istanbul and was now lying in his bed, apparently wearing nothing more than a black choker. Bond and Tania were blissfully unaware that they were being filmed by SPECTRE agents.

MAID in HELL

Bond and Tania had evaded SPECTRE's attempts to ensnare them. They were about to check out of their Venice hotel with the Lektor decoder when there came a knock on the door. A maid entered. Tania recognized her immediately: Rosa Klebb, the Soviet intelligence chief who had recruited her to "give false information to the enemy". In reality, Klebb was a top SPECTRE agent. She pulled a gun, and that's when the trouble started.

Klebb ordered Tania out of the room with the Lektor. She then turned back, aiming her gun at Bond. Klebb was just about to finish SPECTRE's most feared foe, when Tania knocked the gun from her hand.

Horrible woman. Yes. She's had her kicks.

Tania and Bond

A gun wasn't Rosa Klebb's only weapon – she had a poisonous blade in her right shoe. Bond kept her at a distance, and Tania ended Klebb's life with a single shot.

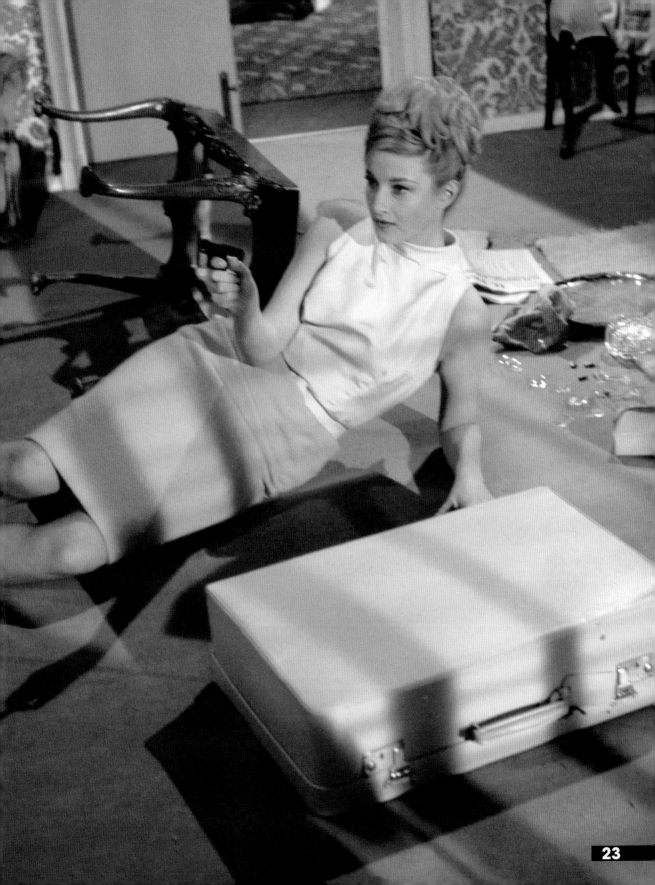

GOLDFINGER ™

Bond has fun catching Auric Goldfinger, one of the world's richest men, cheating at cards but receives a macabre warning: a dead girl covered in gold paint. The Treasury believes Goldfinger is smuggling gold out of the country and M assigns Bond to investigate further. However, the "Man with the Midas touch" has a far more ambitious plan: to irradiate the US gold reserve at Fort Knox with an atomic device and increase the value of his own vast gold store tenfold. He also has a number of unusual uses for a recently acquired industrial laser.

Do you expect me to talk?
No, Mr. Bond. I expect you to die!

Bond and **Goldfinger**

The GOLDEN GIRL

Bond had relished humiliating Auric Goldfinger by catching him cheating at gin rummy. He had thoroughly enjoyed romancing Jill Masterson, Goldfinger's bored, beautiful companion. But now the vibrant girl was a gilded corpse – a chilling warning to Bond not to interfere in Goldfinger's plans again.

The final hole went to Goldfinger, who had cheated his way to victory with help from his caddy Oddjob. But Bond had switched Goldfinger's ball. The fox had been outfoxed.

A ROUND of GOLF

The Bank of England wanted to know how Goldfinger smuggled gold out of the country. The bank loaned Bond tempting bait – a gold ingot worth £5,000 – and Bond met Goldfinger on the golf course. All square and with two holes to go, Goldfinger suggested they play for the ingot. "Strict rules of golf?" "But of course," replied Bond.

This meeting isn't a coincidence, eh?
What's your game, Mr Bond?
My game?
You didn't come here to play golf.

Goldfinger and **Bond**

Bond's DB5 took pride of place outside Goldfinger's golf club.

MOUNTAIN SCENERY

Using a scanner on the dashboard of his Aston Martin DB5, Bond was tracking Goldfinger's Rolls-Royce through twisting Alpine roads. When Goldfinger stopped, so did Bond. A bullet ricocheted near his feet. Bond wondered who it was for.

On the dashboard here, audio-visual. Range one hundred and fifty miles. Ingenious and useful, too. Allow a man to stop off for a quick one en route.

Q and Bond

FLIGHT INTO DANGER

Goldfinger's personal pilot was ice-cool
Pussy Galore. She told Bond they were
heading for Baltimore. Bond, who had
narrowly escaped death at Goldfinger's
hands, needed an edge. By the time they
reached their destination, he had
changed into an impeccably tailored suit
and placed a homer in his shoe.

This should be a memorable flight.
You can turn off the charm – I'm immune.

THUNDERBALL ™

SPECTRE hijacks a bomber carrying two atomic bombs and holds the UK and US to ransom. Bond flies to the Bahamas to find the pilot's sister, Domino Derval. He discovers that her piratical "guardian", Emilio Largo, possesses a yacht, an army of henchmen and a pool full of sharks. He also wears a SPECTRE signet ring.

Domino, I have to tell you something. **You're going away.**
"So sorry, my dear, but it's all over..." No. It's about your
brother... It's a long story. And it involves your friend Largo.

Bond and **Domino Derval**

JET PACK

Was SPECTRE assassin Jacques Boitier dead? MI6 needed to know. Bond observed a "grieving widow" at the funeral and followed her. A chateau became the scene of Boitier's real death – and of Bond's dramatic escape using a Bell-Textron Jet Pack. Agent La Porte helped complete Bond's getaway.

No well-dressed man
should be without one.
Bond

The Bell-Textron Jet Pack was
thought too dangerous by the US
Army. Q Branch appreciated its
potential for agents in tight spots.

Someone has to lose. Yes, I thought I saw a
spectre at your shoulder. **What do you mean?**
The spectre of defeat – that your luck was due to change.

Emilio Largo and Bond

PLAYING with
SPECTRE

Only a few days remained before SPECTRE's ultimatum expired. Not a trace of concern showed on Bond's face as he confronted Emilio Largo across the baccarat table. Did the "guardian" of Domino Derval have something to hide? Perhaps Largo would betray himself with the turn of a losing card...

Seated just behind Largo, Domino watched her new friend James Bond make his play.

YOU ONLY LIVE TWICE

MI6 stage manages Bond's murder and burial at sea in order to convince SPECTRE that its nemesis is finally dead. Before long, Bond is jetting off to Japan to investigate the disappearance of US and Soviet spacecraft. A femme fatale, a Japanese bride, and a volcanic encounter with Ernst Stavro Blofeld, head of SPECTRE, await him. Somehow Bond must stop the US and the USSR being tricked by SPECTRE into starting a third world war.

I've got you now.
Well, enjoy yourself.

Helga Brandt, SPECTRE Number Eleven, and Bond

Miss Moneypenny, chic in a naval uniform, welcomed Bond back to the land of the living.

The DEATH of 007

M knew that Bond's three spectacular victories over SPECTRE had made him a marked man. To throw assassins off the scent, he arranged for Bond to be "murdered" in Hong Kong. Commander Bond was given a traditional naval burial at sea, but the shroud was watertight and he was rescued by divers. And so Bond's "second life" began.

Well, now that you're dead, perhaps some of your old friends will pay a little less attention to you for a while.

M to Bond

NINJA ACADEMY

The search for the enemy base was narrowing to a remote volcanic island. Tiger Tanaka, head of the Japanese secret service, planned an assault with his ninja force. But first, Bond had to undergo not-altogether-painful training at Tanaka's camp, located in picturesque Himeji castle.

During practise with bo staffs, Bond was attacked by a SPECTRE assassin.

Tiger Tanaka and Japanese agent Aki showed Bond an arsenal of unusual weapons used for covert ninja missions, including rocket guns firing jet-propelled bullets.

What's the plan for me?
First you become a Japanese. Second, you train hard and quickly to become a ninja, like us.

Bond and **Tiger Tanaka**

JAPANESE BRIDE

Tanaka's plan for Bond to search for the enemy base in secret required him to masquerade as an Ama fisherman with an Ama wife. Bond was reluctant at first, but he changed his mind when he laid eyes on Kissy Suzuki, the agent Tanaka had chosen to be Bond's Japanese bride.

That is your bed. I shall sleep over there. We're supposed to be married. **Think again, please. You gave false name to priest.**

Kissy Suzuki and Bond

FACE to FACE

Bond had clashed with SPECTRE in the past without ever encountering the organization's ruthless chief, Ernst Stavro Blofeld. That changed when Bond infiltrated Blofeld's rocket base, hidden inside a volcano. After an exchange of pleasantries, Bond found himself staring down the barrel of Blofeld's pistol as the mastermind made his escape.

Allow me to introduce myself. I am Ernst Stavro Blofeld. They told me you were assassinated in Hong Kong. Yes, this is my second life. **You only live twice, Mr. Bond.**

Blofeld and Bond

"Goodbye, Mr. Bond," snarled Blofeld. Before he could pull the trigger, a ninja star thrown by Tiger Tanaka thudded into his gun arm.

ON HER MAJESTY'S SECRET SERVICE™

Bond's mission to hunt down Ernst Stavro Blofeld takes a bizarre turn when crimelord Marc-Ange Draco offers to locate the mastermind if Bond will marry his rebellious daughter Tracy. Already attracted to her, Bond agrees. He exposes Blofeld's plot to visit biological mass murder on the world with his brainwashed "Angels of Death", but Blofeld exacts a terrible revenge, turning the happiest day of Bond's life to tragedy.

I'm relieving you from Operation Bedlam, Double-O-Seven...
You've had two years to run him down.
Does this mean you've lost confidence in me?

M and **Bond**

DRACO'S PROPOSAL

Kidnapped at gunpoint, Bond was in no mood for idle chat when he met Draco, head of the Union Corse. The gang boss only wanted to talk and his urbane manner soon won Bond over. Draco had something Bond wanted: information on Blofeld's whereabouts. Draco's price was distinctly unusual: he wanted Bond to marry his wayward daughter, Tracy. Could a deal be struck? Would Bond become Draco's son-in-law?

Bond and Draco conferred in the boss' luxurious apartment, concealed behind a steel door in a dingy warehouse.

Do not kill me, Mr. Bond. At least not until we've had a drink.

Draco

BOND at BAY

Now, now, now, now, Mr. Bond. You must learn to be absolutely calm before we can accept you back into polite society.

Ernst Stavro Blofeld

Bond's cover was blown and he was at the mercy of his deadliest foe, Ernst Stavro Blofeld, alias the Comte de Bleuchamp. The knowledge Bond had acquired of Blofeld's scheme to control or destroy the economy of the entire world would be useless – unless he could escape.

BOND'S WEDDING

Blofeld was missing, presumed dead. Bond and Tracy were in love – so in love that Bond could laughingly reject her father Draco's offer of a massive dowry. M, Q and Miss Moneypenny wished the happy couple good luck and Mr. and Mrs. James Bond truly believed that they had all the time in the world.

The occasion was an especially emotional one for Miss Moneypenny.

Her price is far above rubies – or even your million pounds.

Bond to Draco

Diamonds Are Forever
Forever
Forever

Bond avenges Tracy's murder by drowning Blofeld in a mud pool in a Cairo clinic. He then embarks on an assignment to discover who is stockpiling smuggled diamonds and why. Bond infiltrates the smuggling pipeline, meets jewel thief Tiffany Case and travels with her to Las Vegas. The stakes are far higher than a case of smuggling. World security is threatened by none other than Blofeld himself, seemingly back from the dead.

Hi, I'm Plenty. **But of course you are.** Plenty O'Toole. **Named after your father, perhaps?**

Plenty O'Toole and **Bond**

You are English? Yes, I'm English. **I speak English. Who is your floor?** Three, please. **Bond** and Peter Franks

A KILLING in old AMSTERDAM

Bond had kept smuggler Peter Franks' appointment with "T. Case". Tipped off by Q that Franks had escaped custody, Bond had to act fast. He intercepted Franks in the lift going up to Tiffany's apartment and, after a brutal struggle, tipped him over a balustrade. A switch of wallets, and the dead Peter Franks became the deceased James Bond.

HOT ICE

The smuggled diamonds were safely in the hands of the CIA's Felix Leiter. Bond could afford to enjoy himself in Las Vegas, the gambling capital of the world. Tiffany Case was happy to enjoy herself, too, but she was even more interested in where the diamonds were.

Why don't we talk a bit first? First? Well, what would you like to talk about? **You pick a subject.** Diamonds? **Good boy!**
Tiffany Case and Bond

LIVE AND LET DIE ™

Sent to New York to investigate the murders of three MI6 agents, Bond mixes in strange and dangerous company, encountering gang boss Mr. Big, the beautiful medium Solitaire, a host of vicious henchmen and Dr. Kananga, the malevolent president of a voodoo-haunted Caribbean island. Bond romances Solitaire and eventually destroys Kananga's scheme to flood the US with cut-price heroin; however, it is Baron Samedi, voodoo God of Death, who has the last laugh.

The legendary Baron Samedi, folks. God of Cemeteries and Chief of the Legion of the Dead. The Man Who Cannot Die.

San Monique hotel MC

VOODOO CULT

A terrifying, deadly ordeal awaited Solitaire on San Monique. Kananga had decreed that she must pay with her life for betraying him and falling for Bond: she should become a human sacrifice to voodoo death god Baron Samedi. Kananga believed her ritual murder would warn others not to incur his displeasure. Kananga had reckoned without Bond.

Bond had disposed of a dummy Baron Samedi. Now he faced the machete-wielding real thing.

Seems like the party's started.
Bond

SCENTING BLOOD

Bond's solo attempt to save Solitaire and destroy Kananga's poppy fields seemed to have ended in disaster. He and Solitaire were imprisoned in Kananga's underground bunker, dangling helplessly over a pool of hungry sharks. Then Bond remembered the watch given to him by Q, with its magnetic field and buzz-saw bezel.

I'm sure there must be a simpler way of drowning someone.
Drown, Mr. Bond? I doubt you get the chance to drown...

Bond and *Kananga*

The buzz-saw in Bond's watch cut him free. Bond wrestled Kananga into his own shark pool and pushed a compressed-air bullet into his mouth. Kananga literally blew up.

69

THE MAN WITH THE GOLDEN GUN™

A gold bullet inscribed "007" – the calling card of Francisco Scaramanga, the world's foremost assassin – arrives at MI6. Bond pursues Scaramanga around South-East Asia following gold bullets and encountering Scaramanga's doomed girlfriend Andrea Anders. With help – and hindrance – from MI6 agent Mary Goodnight, Bond tracks down Scaramanga and duels to the death in his Fun House.

Who would pay a million dollars to have me killed?
Jealous husbands, outraged chefs, humiliated

The dojo's sensei chose his prize pupil Chula to be Bond's opponent. Bond found his most effective ploy was an old-fashioned right hook to the jaw.

KARATE SCHOOL

Captured by Hai Fat, Bond awoke to find himself the centre of unwelcome attention. It seemed that he was the guest of honour, or rather the sacrificial lamb, at a meeting of a karate dojo. Bond knew he would need quick wits as well as all his unarmed combat skills to get out in one piece.

Schoolgirl karate experts Cha and Nara covered Bond's escape by defeating Hai Fat's entire karate school.

FUN HOUSE
DUEL

The Fun House was a disorienting hall of mirrors that Scaramanga used to hone his assassin's skills. The "attraction" was peopled by gun-toting mannequins – there was even a dummy James Bond, Scaramanga's tribute to MI6's finest. Scaramanga now had the chance to pit himself against the real thing. Only one of them would emerge from the Fun House alive.

A duel between titans.
My Golden Gun against
your Walther PPK.
Six bullets to your one?
I only need one.

Scaramanga and **Bond**

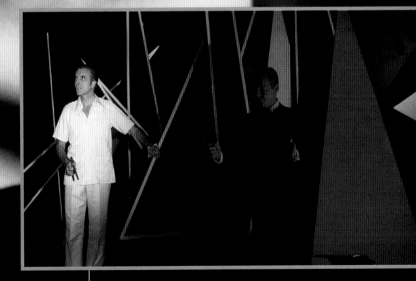

Bond decided that the best way to defeat Scaramanga was to hide in plain sight – as his own mannequin.

THE SPY WHO LOVED ME™

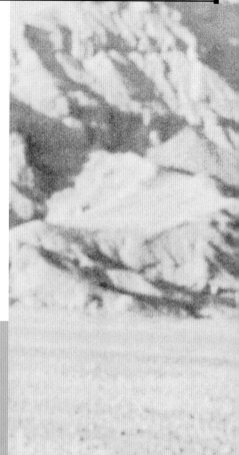

Bond and Major Anya Amasova, Agent Triple X of the KGB, join forces to investigate Karl Stromberg, a power-crazed shipping magnate who dreams of ruling a "new and beautiful world" beneath the sea. Battling gigantic, steel-toothed hitman Jaws as well as Stromberg's private army, Bond and Anya foil a plot to use hijacked nuclear submarines to bring about global devastation. The two agents then have their own differences to settle.

Thanks for deserting me back there.
Every woman for herself – remember?
Still – you *did* save my life.
We all make mistakes, Mr. Bond.

Bond and Anya

BOND of ARABIA

Sheik Hosein treated Bond to his own brand of traditional Arab hospitality. "We don't only have oil, you know."

What can I offer you? Sheep's eyes? Dates? Vodka Martini? **Information.** What a pity you insist on being so businesslike.

Sheik Hosein and **Bond**

A top-secret submarine tracking system was on sale in Cairo to the highest bidder. Assigned to get hold of it, Bond donned burnous, ghutra and aghal – traditional Arab dress – jumped on a camel and set off across the desert to visit Sheik Hosein, MI6's Egyptian contact. The Sheik was an old friend of Bond's from his student days at Cambridge.

BITING BACK

In the ruins of an ancient temple, Jaws, the man mountain who had seized the microfilm of the submarine tracking system for Karl Stromberg, played cat and mouse with Bond and Anya. He attacked Bond, and Anya saw her chance to claim the microfilm for the KGB.

MOONRAKER™

A stolen space shuttle sends Bond on the track of the shuttle's manufacturer, aerospace magnate Hugo Drax. With trained astronaut Holly Goodhead of the CIA, Bond must somehow foil Drax's plan to decimate humanity from his secret space station and repopulate the world with his own master race.

Moonraker 5 – that's the answer. Drax's shuttle is armed with a laser. We can track those globes and destroy them.

Bond

LOCKED OUT

Bond had shattered Drax's god-like dream of a beautiful new world with himself as ruler. His space station was under attack – again Bond's doing. Retaining his customary composure, Drax aimed a gun at his nemesis, savouring the moment with a final witticism: "At least I shall have the pleasure of putting you out of my misery." Before Drax could fire, he felt a sudden shooting pain in his heart.

At the start of the Moonraker mission, Q had presented Bond with a wrist dart gun, activated by nerve impulses.

Drax assumed that Bond was helpless, but with a flick of the wrist Bond fired his dart gun. Drax staggered backwards. Bond opened the airlock and sent Drax cartwheeling into space.

Take a giant step for mankind!
Bond

FLOATING in SPACE

Thanks to Dr. Holly Goodhead's piloting skills and Bond's expert aiming, Hugo Drax's masterplan to wipe out the peoples of Earth with globes of nerve gas had spectacularly failed. The world was safe, at least for the time being, and Bond and Holly felt like they were walking on air.

By the time Bond and Holly reached Drax's space station, they had buried their differences to become a formidable team.

FOR YOUR EYES ONLY ™

Bond faces double-dealing and merciless savagery in the Mediterranean on a mission involving a shipwreck, a top-secret ATAC transmitter, a beautiful, passionate avenger named Melina Havelock and rival kingpins in the Greek underworld, Aris Kristatos and Milos Columbo. One of these gangsters is a potential ally and one is a sadistic manipulator in the pay of the KGB. Before too long, Bond discovers which is which.

I didn't think it would end like this.
We're not dead yet.

Melina and **Bond**

GRAVE MATTERS

Bond rarely mentioned that he had once been married. The memory of beautiful, vivacious Tracy di Vicenzo, gunned down on their wedding day, was still painfully fresh in his mind. He was standing lost in thought by her gravestone, inscribed with their favourite saying, "We have all the time in the world", when a priest informed him that his "office" was sending a helicopter to pick him up. Was there something suspicious about the priest's manner?

TERESA BOND
1943 · 1969
Beloved Wife of
JAMES BOND
We have all the
time in the World

ASSAULT on ST. CYRIL'S

Bond's resolve to prevent the invaluable ATAC transmitter from falling into Soviet hands resulted in one of his most dangerous and arduous exploits: scaling single-handed the almost vertical cliff leading to St. Cyril's monastery, the lair of crime kingpin and KGB agent Aris Kristatos.

Melina, Columbo and his men looked on anxiously as Bond inched his way up the cliff, towards Kristatos' stronghold.

Kristatos believed his stronghold was impregnable. Bond had other ideas.

OCTOPUSSY™

A fake Fabergé egg sends Bond to India on the trail of shady art dealer Kamal Khan. Bond meets the fabulously wealthy jewel smuggler Octopussy with her female army, Floating Palace and travelling circus, and exposes a rogue Soviet general's plot to explode a nuclear bomb in West Germany and invade Europe.

On James. We're two of a kind. There are vast rewards for a man of your talents willing to take risks.
I'm not for hire.

Octopussy and **Bond**

Pay attention,
Double-O-Seven!

Q

The earpiece in Bond's pen was linked to a homing device-cum-microphone small enough to fit into the coach in a Fabergé egg.

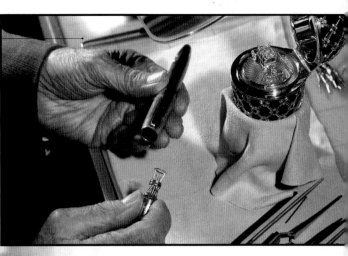

Q in DELHI

The poster of a winged serpent hid the entrance to Q's Delhi lab. Q was "most unhappy" to see Double-O-Seven. "How can I be expected to maintain the quality of my work? Sent out here at a moment's notice. No proper facilities..." Nevertheless, Q had brought several items to help Bond investigate Kamal Khan, including a pen containing acid and an earpiece linked to a homer/mic – useful for escape and also surveillance.

CIRCUS of FEAR

Before Bond's timely intervention, Octopussy, a US general and his aide and Kamal Khan (shortly to depart) thought the show was a blast.

General, there's a bomb in that cannon!
Bond

The human cannonball proved the climax of the evening – in more ways than one.

The harmless hilarity of Octopussy's circus concealed a ticking bomb. General Orlov's insane plan to set off a nuclear bomb as an apocalyptic prelude to European invasion looked certain of success. With only seconds to spare, Bond, dressed in a stolen clown suit, charged into the ring.

A VIEW TO A KILL ™

In Siberia, Bond recovers a supposedly secret British microchip from the body of an MI6 agent. The chip's manufacturer, Max Zorin, is suspected of fixing horse races, but he has far greater ambitions. Abetted by his assassin lover May Day, Zorin is prepared to go to any lengths to control the world market in microchips, including the total destruction of California's Silicon Valley.

Unbelievable. In all my years as a trainer, I've never seen a horse run such a fast last furlong.

Sir Godfrey Tibbett

An ASSASSIN in PARIS

Death in the shape of a masked assassin stalked the Eiffel Tower's Jules Verne restaurant and a detective with valuable information about Max Zorin lay dead. Bond pursued the black-clad figure up the Eiffel Tower. Surely there was no way the killer could escape?

The elusive killer's identity was
a mystery Bond was determined
to crack. But first he – or she –
had to be caught.

May Day was sure she had seen Bond somewhere before and alerted Zorin.

HIGH SOCIETY

A swell party at Zorin's stud farm presented Bond with the ideal opportunity to find out more about the microchip mogul and his shady associates. Posing as race horse owner James St. John Smythe, Bond ruffled a few feathers, before an attractive woman in blue caught his eye. Bond had just witnessed Zorin handing her a cheque for $5 million, yet she looked anything but happy.

Hello. I thought you might like to join the party. By the way, my name is James St. John Smythe.

Bond to Stacey Sutton

THE LIVING DAYLIGHTS™

During a training exercise, Agent 004 winds up dead with a note in Russian "Smiert Spionam" ("Death to Spies") near his body. Have the the KGB revived a Stalinist murder campaign? Bond believes that beautiful cello-virtuoso-turned-assassin Kara Milovy holds the key. As the body count of British agents rises, Bond uncovers a plot involving a faked defection, a power struggle within the KGB, a war-obsessed arms dealer and a massive weapons-for-drugs deal in Afghanistan.

Who are you? **Bond. James Bond. Exercise Control? Double-O-Seven here. I'll report in an hour.** Won't you join me? **Better make that two.**

Linda and **Bond**

DEATH on the ROCK

The SAS have been placed on full alert to intercept you, but I know you won't let me down. Good luck, men!

M

Bond hurled himself onto the roof of a hijacked British army Land Rover as the killer made his escape.

Spotted by an SAS guard, the Smiert Spionam assassin returned fire with a bullet, not paint. He then cut short Agent 004's life.

It was supposed to be just a training exercise with nothing more than the pride of the Service at stake. Three Double-O agents, Bond among them, had to penetrate Gibraltar's radar defences, avoiding SAS guards armed with nothing more deadly than paintball guns. But the exercise had been infiltrated by an assassin with a very different agenda.

Kara Milovy, Koskov's former girlfriend had to decide whose side she was on. She soon made up her mind.

AIRBASE ATTACK

Bond had been kidnapped and imprisoned on a Soviet base in Afghanistan, but now was his time to hit back. Treacherous KGB general Georgi Koskov and his comrades suddenly found the tables had turned as mujaheddin tribesmen led by Kamran Shah launched a surprise attack. Bond hijacked Koskov's cargo plane and a lucrative drugs-for-arms deal began to show signs of unravelling.

You can't leave him. You owe him your life.

Kara Milovy to
Kamran Shah

Koskov, the airbase commander and the assassin Necros took cover as the bullets flew.

LICENCE TO KILL ™

Against M's orders and with his licence to kill revoked, Bond goes after drug baron Franz Sanchez, responsible for mutilating Felix Leiter and murdering Della, Leiter's bride. Bond finds important allies in intrepid ex-CIA pilot Pam Bouvier and MI6's own Q as he seeks to bring down Sanchez' organization and avenge his friends.

He disagreed with something that ate him.
Note left on Leiter's body by Franz Sanchez

If they start shooting, hit the deck and stay there.

Pam Bouvier to Bond

HONKY-TONK ANGEL

The patrons of the Barrelhead Bar enjoyed a ruckus. They joined in enthusiastically when Bond and Pam Bouvier clashed with Sanchez's enforcer Dario and his buddies. Fortunately, Pam had brought along a pump-action shotgun to even up the odds.

Amid the chaos, Pam blasted a hole in the wall with her shotgun, allowing Bond to escape and start up his boat.

FAMILY REUNION

Bond's licence to kill had been revoked by M, but he still had friends in the Service – none more loyal than the sometimes-irascible Q. Realizing Bond would need help to take down Sanchez, Q showed up in Isthmus City with a bag full of tricks.

Remember – if it hadn't been for Q Branch, you'd have been dead long ago.

Q to Bond

GOLDENEYE ™

A Tiger helicopter, proof against electromagnetism, is hijacked and employed to steal the GoldenEye satellite weapons system from a Siberia research station. GoldenEye's electromagnetic pulse then obliterates the station. M suspects the Janus crime syndicate and, after a clear-the-air-meeting with her top agent, sends Bond to St. Petersburg to investigate. Bond encounters an old friend believed killed in action: Alex Trevelyan, formerly Agent 006… an old friend with a fierce grudge against Britain, Bond and everything he stands for.

You don't like me, Bond. You don't like my methods. You think I'm an accountant, a bean counter, more interested in my numbers than your instincts.

The thought had occurred to me.
Good. Because I think you're a sexist, misogynist dinosaur, a relic of the Cold War…

M and *Bond*

For England, James!

Alec Trevelyan, Agent 006

THE BEST of ENEMIES

The MI6 mission to penetrate and destroy a Soviet chemical weapons factory in Arkangel was going smoothly. Too smoothly for Bond's liking. His fears were confirmed when troops led by General Ourumov captured his brother-in-arms Alec Trevelyan. A tense stand-off later, Ourumov appeared to shoot Trevelyan in the head and Bond was in the fight of his life to escape.

Bond and Alec Trevelyan were friends – or so Bond believed. But the mission was an elaborate hoax to allow Trevelyan to fake his own death and bring about Bond's capture.

Walther PPK 7.65 millimetre. Only three men I know use such a gun. I believe I've killed two of them. Lucky me.

Valentin Zukovsky and Bond

PROFESSIONAL COURTESY

One man in St. Petersburg could arrange a meeting with Janus: ex-KGB agent, now crime boss and fixer *par excellence* Valentin Zukovsky. Years before, Bond had shot Zukovsky in the leg, stolen his car and taken his girl. An appeal to his heart was out of the question. Bond hoped an appeal to his wallet would suffice.

Zukovsky now had a new girlfriend, Irina, a would-be singer. "Who's strangling the cat?" enquired Bond.

TomorrowNeverDies

™

A British warship, wildly off course, sinks with all hands, sparking an international incident with China. The story is a massive scoop for the Carver Media Group Network owned by Elliot Carver. Bond's efforts to check up on the power-crazed media mogul are met with ruthless violence. Bond teams up with Chinese agent Wai Lin to foil Carver's plan to bring about war between Britain and China, wipe out the Chinese high command, and gain exclusive Chinese satellite transmission rights for his network.

We're going to finish this together.

Bond to Wai Lin

ONE-MAN ARMY

M looked on as cameras beamed back pictures of the "terrorist supermarket" to MI6.

Admiral Roebuck, impatient with M's "softly-softly", information-gathering approach, wanted direct action. Bond supplied it, making the Admiral look a fool in the process.

Bond's mission was to infiltrate a terrorist arms bazaar on the Russian border and identify the key participants. Admiral Roebuck had other ideas, and recklessly ordered a missile strike. Bond indicated that one of the fighter planes was carrying nuclear torpedoes. A disaster that would make Chernobyl look like a picnic was inevitable – unless Bond could battle his way to that plane and fly it out of there.

White Knight to White Rook.
I've evacuated the area. Ask the Admiral
where he'd like his bombs delivered.

Bond

Moments before
the missile struck, Bond
flew off in the L39
Albatross carrying the
nuclear torpedoes.

TEARING HURRY

Captured and threatened with torture, Bond and Chinese agent Wai Lin had to escape Carver's clutches. Only problem: they were on top of a skyscraper and handcuffed together. With a brilliant piece of smash and grab, Bond and Wai Lin exploited these disadvantages, sliding to freedom down an enormous poster of Carver's face.

Elliot Carver promised to use chakra torture on Bond and Wai Lin. This technique inflicted "the maximum amount of pain whilst keeping the victim alive as long as possible."

We can use
the banner.
Hope it holds.
Ready? Go!

Wai Lin

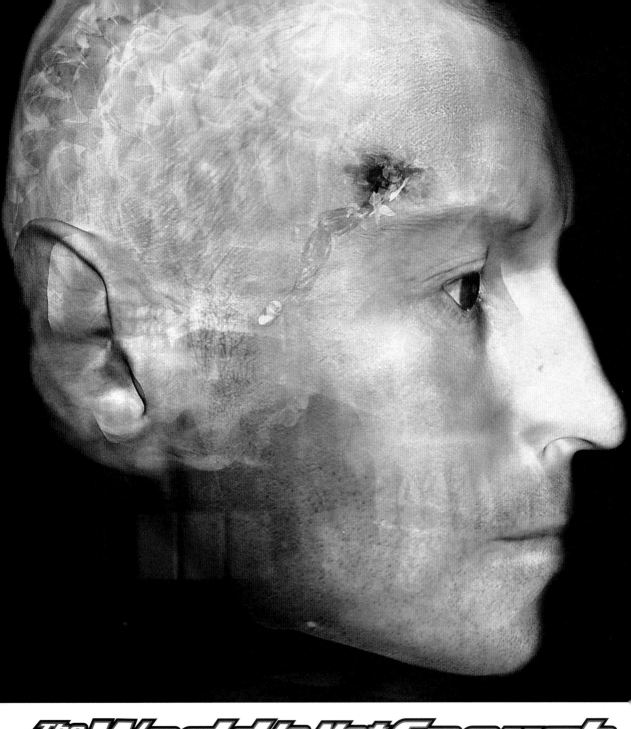

British oil magnate Sir Robert King is blown up right inside MI6 Thameside headquarters. The chief suspect is the anarchist and terrorist Renard, living on borrowed time with a bullet lodged in his brain. M and Bond become convinced that King's daughter Elektra is Renard's next target. Assigned to shadow Elektra, Bond discovers that her beauty and fiery independence conceal a much, much darker side.

Renard, the anarchist.
He was operating in Moscow in 1999; Pyongyang, North Korea, before that; and he's been spotted in Afghanistan, Bosnia, Iraq, Iran, and Beirut and Cambodia.
Hmm. All the romantic vacation spots.

Bond and Tanner, MI6 senior analyst

Lachaise's secretary supplied Bond with a set of "perfectly rounded" figures. She also had another talent: assassination.

REVERSAL of FORTUNE

Bond had little affection for Swiss bankers, especially unscrupulous ones like Lachaise, involved by association in blackmail, terror threats and the murder of a British agent. As well as collecting a case full of cash belonging to industrialist Sir Robert King, Bond wanted information: the name of the killer.

I'm giving you the opportunity to walk out with your life.

Bond

Bond evaded the Spanish police by securing a rope to the body of one of Lachaise's henchmen and abseiling to the pavement.

DEATH and the MAIDEN

Elektra King possessed enough brains, beauty and charm to bewitch anyone – and she knew it. Despite his instincts, and M's orders, Bond fell under her spell. But faced with deciding whether she was worth the lives of millions of innocent people, Bond did not hesitate.

> You wouldn't kill me.
> You'd miss me.
> **I never miss.**
>
> Elektra King and **Bond**

Elektra had the chance to call off Renard's atomic bomb plot. She gambled that Bond wouldn't pull the trigger.

A single bullet from Bond's gun took Elektra's life.

135

DIE ANOTHER DAY

Captured and tortured when a mission in North Korea is compromised, Bond goes it alone to clear his name. He hunts a terrorist in Cuba, encounters sultry CIA agent Jinx, and finds a vital diamond clue. Back in favour with M, Bond investigates mysterious diamond magnate Gustav Graves, a man who claims to dream of creating a better world. But Graves is not what he seems, and his dreams are the stuff of nightmares.

Still you jest. Defiant to the last. Your people have abandoned you.

General Moon

So what do predators do when the sun goes down? **They feast – like there's no tomorrow.**

Jinx and **Bond**

CUBA LIBRE

Bond was in Cuba to track down the terrorist Zao. However, the sight of the girl rising gracefully from the waves was too arresting to pass by. Zao could wait. The girl called herself Jinx, and she had more in common with Bond than he realized. Like him, she was a secret agent. Like him, she had an evening to kill.

Bond was surveying the clinic of a certain Dr. Alvarez, where Zao was having treatment. Then he noticed Jinx.

So this is where they keep the old relics…

I'll have you know this is where our most cutting-edge technology is developed.

Bond and **Q**

PAST and FUTURE

MI6's new Quartermaster proved just as ready to bandy words with Double-O-Seven, and just as serious about his work as his illustrious predecessor. He showed Bond into his lab, which contained souvenirs of many of Bond's missions.

Bond couldn't resist checking whether the Jet Pack from his Thunderball assignment was still working. It was.

FLASHING BLADES

Bond's Cuban adventure had thrown up a clue – an African conflict diamond inscribed with the mark of Gustav Graves. Was the glamorous, well-connected, immensely wealthy Graves, a newly-appointed knight of the realm, dealing in illegal diamonds? Bond went to meet the man known as "The King of Diamonds" at his fencing club – and one thing led to another…

As Graves lost his temper, the niceties of fencing were forgotten, and his duel with Bond became a battle.

Let's do this the old-fashioned way. First blood drawn from the torso.

Gustav Graves

CASINO ROYALE

Bond gains his licence to kill and lays his life on the line foiling an airport bomb plot. The man behind the scheme is banker-to-terrorists Le Chiffre, and M sends Bond to defeat him at poker at Montenegro's famed Casino Royale. Much more awaits Bond there than just a high-stakes gambling game. Intrigue, treachery, pain and heartbreak lie in the turn of a card.

I'm not gonna last much longer. You've a better chance.
I'll stake you… Just one thing: if you pull it off, the CIA bring him in.
And what about the winnings?
Does it look like we need the money?

WINNER TAKES ALL

Le Chiffre had done his best, or rather worst, to eliminate Bond from the game. Now, with the digitalis antidote kicking in, Bond was ready for the final phase. He had promised Vesper he could defeat Le Chiffre. Now was the time to prove it.

The five cards face up in front of Bond looked distinctly unpromising. Confident that his full house would win, Le Chiffre called Bond with $115 million at stake.

Oh, I'm sorry.
That last hand…
Nearly killed me.
Bond

SHEER TORTURE

The time for playing games was over. Bond knew that Le Chiffre had to have the password to the bank account holding the winnings. Otherwise Le Chiffre was a dead man. As Bond fought the pain, he clung to the thought that, if he died, at least he would take Le Chiffre with him.

It's the simplest thing to cause more pain than a man can possibly endure.

Le Chiffre

Vesper could see no way out. Trapped in a lift inside a collapsing Venetian villa, overcome with despair at her betrayal of Bond and her country, she decided there was only one way to end her suffering.

Vesper Lynd saw through the "007, Licensed to Kill" bravura Bond liked to project. He sensed she was hiding something, that something was eating away at her, and the thought brought out a protective side he didn't realize he possessed. He was even prepared to resign from the Service to be with her. Bond couldn't know that malign forces had doomed their relationship from their first meeting to their last.

BOND and VESPER

"Whatever is left, whatever I am…
I am yours."

Bond

QUANTUM OF SOLACE

SOLACE

7

Embittered by Vesper Lynd's betrayal, Bond goes after Quantum, the insidious organization that made her turn traitor. Bond's target is Quantum agent Dominic Greene and his scheme to control Bolivia's water supply. Bond finds an ally in the beautiful but feisty Camille, and, at last, answers to the questions tormenting him.

The first thing you should know about us is that we have people *everywhere*.

Mr. White

BLACK
DEATH

I think you're so blinded by inconsolable rage, you don't care who you hurt.

M to Bond

She had bravely backed Bond. Now Agent Fields had paid with her life – drowned in crude oil, black gold that was supposed to lie beneath the Bolivian desert. M blamed Bond for her death, but Bond knew where the blame really lay – with Dominic Greene and the Quantum organization.

Greene's veneer of sophistication vanished as he saw his scheme to plunder Bolivia's natural resources literally go up in smoke.

BLAZING FURY

The Perla de las Dunas hotel was a raging inferno. All Bond's pent-up anger at Quantum and its machinations finally exploded as he got to grips with the Machiavellian CEO of Greene Planet, Dominic Greene.

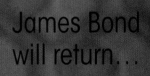

James Bond
will return…

LONDON, NEW YORK,
MUNICH, MELBOURNE
AND DELHI

Designed by Dan Bunyan
for Dorling Kindersley

Senior Editor Alastair Dougall
Senior Designer Lynne Moulding
Managing Editor Catherine Saunders
Art Director Lisa Lanzarini
Publishing Manager Simon Beecroft
Category Publisher Alex Allan
Production Editor Clare McLean
Production Controller Nick Seston

First published in Great Britain in 2010
by Dorling Kindersley Limited, 80 Strand, London, WC2R 0RL

10 11 12 13 10 9 8 7 6 5 4 3 2 1
177921 – 02/10

Compilation copyright © 2010 Dorling Kindersley Limited

A CIP catalogue record for this book is available from the British Library

ISBN: 978-1-4053-5534-6

Colour reproduction by Alta Image, London
Printed and bound in China Leo Paper Products

Discover more at www.dk.com

The author and Dorling Kindersley would like to thank Jenni McMurrie
of EON Productions for her invaluable help during the production of this book.